Prais

A highly distinctive poet. His work as a translator would be impressive enough, but he is also a poet of power and skill in his own right, currently concentrating on the sonnet. He is a writer of the "plain style", a style arguably more difficult to employ because it lacks the dazzle of rhetoric which can be confused for poetry.   – *Gerry Cambridge*

It is good to be reminded, by this substantial collection of sonnets, of the continued pleasure which is still to be obtained from metre and rhyme. Good observation, spiced with moments of black humour and social satire, makes this a book to be relished for its unexpectedness.   – *Edwin Morgan*

The sonnet 'Two Boys' wields a force available only to a writer who understands the structural potential of this poetic form inside out. It made me cry. I regard Dick Davis's 'Baucis and Philemon' as the great sonnet of my generation, and I hope that in Stocks we are seeing Davis's worthy heir in the making.   – *Timothy Murphy*

Mike Stocks's poems are part of a general humane concern for the disruptions, pleasures and ironies of ordinary life… He is in firm command of his various forms, but not in such a tyrannical way that the poems simply march to order… physically vivid, inventive, but controlled by manners of line, breath, cadence and rhyme.   – *George Szirtes*

Folly

MIKE STOCKS

HERLA

Published by
HERLA PUBLISHING, an imprint of

ALMA BOOKS LTD
London House
243–253 Lower Mortlake Road
Richmond
Surrey TW9 2LL
United Kingdom
www.almabooks.com

Folly first published by Herla, an imprint of Alma Books Ltd, in 2006
Copyright © Mike Stocks, 2006

Mike Stocks asserts his moral right to be identified as the author of this
work in accordance with the Copyright, Designs and Patents Act 1988

Printed in Jordan by the National Press

ISBN-13: 978-1-84688-020-9
ISBN-10: 1-84688-020-3

To Sana

Thanks to the editors of the following publications,
where some of the poems in this book have appeared:

*Chapman, The Dark Horse, The Eildon Tree,
The Evelyn Waugh Studies Newsletter, Magma,
New Writing Scotland 21, Poetry Nottingham, Worm*

Folly

Two Boys

However it may be that those two boys
decided to explore the disused shaft,
and whether it was someone's taunting laugh
that egged them on, or just their own "ahoy"s

echoing back to them – they went ahead,
and three days later rescue teams went down
and found them curled together underground,
and one was still alive, and one was dead.

The fathers waiting at the top were told,
but didn't know whose boy was quarry-cold
until the live one was brought out at last,

and when they saw him both of them collapsed
like slaughtered stock. And you will never see
a man held by a man so helplessly.

Everything in Its Place

It's not that I'm against domestic bliss,
but you two, with your his-'n-hers cagouls
and coffee cups, your shiny garden tools
and geometric lawn, you're taking this

too far, it does my head in when you lean
your mountain bikes against the blossom tree
and scrub the spokes down individually
with last year's toothbrushes until they gleam –

I'm warning you, you've got beneath my skin,
my sleep's all shot, I can't stop thinking of
the equidistant bedside table lights

inside the master bedroom of your love,
and then that penis, slotting neatly in,
like something one should put away at night.

Blame It on the Sun

The question with the answer no one knows
is lying hard at hand in all this air
that holds me here, hot on the folding chair
I carried down, as children trade slack blows

on the warm grass and tired women doze
like seals at noon, their dimpled blubber bared
and proffered to the oldest god up there.
The question with no answer ebbs and flows

down all this long and easy Saturday,
and never mind the frisbee sailing in
above the happy boy – come what may

that's how it is, despite your love for me,
regardless of the hours that underpin
what's left of everyone and everything.

Café Owner on the Royal Mile

I know your game you dirty little man,
the way you advertise for foreign girls
– language students, teenies seeing the world –
and pick the freshest, breastiest you can.

What else explains the waitresses you get?
Each beauty stays a month and then she's gone,
supplanted by the latest gorgeous one
to slip into your grubby little net.

Don't men apply for work occasionally?
Or average girls, with average breasts and faces?
Can't you run things on a fairer basis?

No waitresses could be less use than these,
their coffee is like piss and so's their tea
and – yes, another cappuccino please.

Argument

The pillow's damp tonight from too much weeping,
and all the arm's-length anger of your hair
is stretched from over here to over there.
I lie awake and listen to your sleeping.

This is a strange relationship we're keeping,
a borrowed crop we trample and repair,
and both of us are overly aware
such damage makes for an uncertain reaping.

Each night you worry what the day will bring,
and that I don't believe in anything,
and that it isn't true that absence of

belief in things is more like love than love,
and I – I stroke them in the darkness there,
your hundred thousand filaments of hair.

Princes Street Gardens

A dog with one leg missing sniffed a trail
across the park that shadows Princes Street,
and as I thought about his three small feet
I saw a blackbird with a mangled tail.

A flightless bird, a dog that couldn't run –
and neither thinking why, nor knowing more,
and not the dog and not the blackbird saw
my damaged human being looking on.

Count all the crimes for which there's no forgiving,
each forest felled, a million species lost,
the violence done and now the coming cost,

but nature is the cruel conformist place,
and only the human world allots a space
in which the broken beasts can scratch a living.

Lexicography

Here a word is stalked across
the terrain of its intent
like an old rhinoceros

harried round a continent
by some hearty hairy hale
conservationist, each sense

picked up like a scent and trailed.

I defined the sea today
with exact professional pride,
while the oceans washed away

with their waters and their tides
and their influential past
at the island's brittle sides.

Definitions will not last.

Piano Stool in Tollcross

At times the minor gods put on a show,
like when we lugged your piano stool across
that mean old Friday-nighter in Tollcross,
and you remembered we'd been running low

on contraception since two weeks ago,
and passing Woolies (open until ten
and very cheap on Durex) in we went,
hand in handle with your stool in tow,

and umm-ed and aah-ed the condoms thoughtfully,
while a guard who'd seen most things before
subjected us to extra scrutiny

and conjured up this vision – you, and me,
cavorting with our purchase from that store –
and wondered what the piano stool was for.

Junior Doctor in the Western General

At times the minor gods must get depressed,
like when your knackered colleague got a bleep
about a sudden cardiac arrest,
so giving up his urgent need for sleep

(and newly qualified to do his best)
he sprinted to the distant ARU
like someone hippocraticly possessed,
but then the sole came slipping off his shoe

and flip-flap-flopped the flooring noisily,
so when he reached that grave emergency
– a dying man, the frantic CPR –

the doctors and the nurses went too far,
laughing (while they worked) until they cried,
and couldn't save the dying man, who died.

Lunch

Pathetic, devastated, and in love,
I went to work that day with stupid things:
toothpaste, toothbrush, soap, some stuff for shaving,
an extra shirt I'd ironed the hell out of

at 6 a.m., some hair gel, and a comb.
I faked a morning's work convincingly,
the way I'd faked each long day since you left me,
then took my stupid booty to the bathroom.

We met for lunch. And just one week, was it,
since you'd turned my world a freezing black?
We talked across your high new walls of granite,

and nothing I could be could get you back.
(Pathetic, that I'd put such high hopes in
a crisply ironed shirt, a twice-shaved chin.)

To a Dog Tied to a Tree in the High Street

All passing ankles are superfluous
but those that hinge onto your Owner's knees,
knees suspended from such happy thighs
as have the fortune to support no less

than His triumphant torso (which His head
ecstatically tops off). You foolish dog –
there's stranger things to whine about than legs
that don't connect to Him, so sniff this blood

which spots that tree. There was a fight last night.
Two men lashed out for nothing much, while blue
with cold the girl looked on, as pigeons slept,

as cars drove past, as puddles captured light
then gave it back. When morning came it swept
the street with work. And the tree, dog, grew.

The Archetypal Hypochondriac

The archetypal hypochondriac,
no piles were playing up like yours, no veins
were quite so varicose, and no bad back
had ever dealt such martyr-making pain.

You paralysed the neighbourhood with fear.
I seldom ventured out for milk or eggs
in case you pounced and bent back both my ears
with epics on your scabietic legs.

And now you've had a massive heart attack –
fantastic! Neighbours draw their curtains back,
and bask within the light, and wave at me

who's walking shopwards with impunity.
I even share a giggle with your wife
as oh dear me you fight to bend back life.

Miscast

Since you were caught with trousers at half-mast,
your loose and snowy buttocks rippling as
you spasmed up a nice young man's tight ass,
the vague contempt you had for me has passed,

and now your wife has thrown you out at last –
not because you are a man who has
been caught with half your dick up that crevasse,
but for the lies you told her thick and fast,

you think that I'm disgusted and aghast,
but you don't know about my own morass
of furtive acts and lies and all that jazz,

in which I too am an enthusiast,
nor that my life's as prepossessing as
your average dank and piss-pooled underpass.

Describing a Horse

Just a rained-on nag beneath a rowan tree
you are, gamely stamping now and nearly dead,
a clapped-out nag, but once a thoroughbred
that romped to half a dozen local victories.

My choice full words can't help you to survive.
There should be other poetries, powerful
and harsh and meritless, unreadable,
but able to insist a horse alive –

It is a horse it is a horse it is
a horse it is a horse it is a horse
it is a horse it is a horse… It is,

but not for long beneath the rain, the rowan.
There is an absence galloping the course
and overtaking horse rain tree me poem.

Letters from a Dead Writer

Birthday suicide, your letters landing
gingerly like tiny probes from the far
system of being dead, were these your
finest stories, taut, crafted, demanding

and receiving awed attention, and sending
all who read them shocked and reeling through
the dumb if-onlys and what-ifs that you
bequeath to them with such a killer ending?

They say a Sunday Magazine might run
a story on the story you've become,
and that a film director wants to see

if there's potential in your life's abyss;
they say that hacks you hardly knew – like me –
will use you for material – like this.

Life of Man

from the romanesco of La vita dell'omo,
by Giuseppe Gioacchino Belli

Nine months in a swamp, then swaddling clothes
and sloppy kisses, rashes, big round tears,
a baby harness, baby walker, bows,
short trousers and a cap for several years,

and then begin the agonies of school,
the ABC, the pox, the six of the best,
the poo-poo in the pants, the ridicule,
the chilblains, measles, fevers on the chest;

then work arrives, the daily slog, the rent,
the fasts, the stretch inside, the government,
the hospitals, the debts to pay, the fucks...

The chaser to it all, on God's say-so,
(after summer's sun and winter's snow)
is death, and after death comes hell – life sucks.

The Fruits of the Sermon

from the romanesco of Er frutto de la predica,
by Giuseppe Gioacchino Belli

So having read the gospel, there and then
that good and learned father plonked his rear
against the altarpiece, and – crystal-clear –
explained the mysteries of faith to men;

oh yes, expounded on them inside out,
and every which way told us what they are,
and gave us explanations, more by far
than hundreds, to address our every doubt.

He cited parables, an awful lot,
and gave interpretations, reams and reams,
just like a crystal-gazer of your dreams.

In short, and from this sermon that we got,
to sum it up, to say it how it is,
it seems that mysteries are mysteries.

Lard

from the romanesco of Li connimenti,
by Giuseppe Gioacchino Belli

Yeah, when it comes to cooking, lard's the best.
Matter of fact, my barber said it could
do wonders for the health, a power of good,
like pepper – puts some hairs upon your chest!

With bacon it's a dream, with rarebits it's
the business, chicken too, and roasted meat,
and as for stews and sauces, works a treat –
but using it to fry in, that's the pits.

You're up for frying fish in lard? You'll spoil
it, whitebait should be fried in olive oil,
your olive oil's the stuff for frying fish.

Delicious! Oh I'm nuts about that dish,
and so's the Pope, just look at him, so fat –
he licks it off his whiskers like a cat.

Age

I wouldn't gladly take your age to bed
and nonchalantly sleep with it, my head
      supported on its casual arm,
        my breathing regular and calm.

Your age regards you as its bit of fluff,
its nightly duplicated one-night stand
to which, each night, it feels less passionate.
      No matter how you cling to it

      you will not hold it hard enough,
nor stop it slipping from those sleeping hands.
One day it rises early in that room it knows,

        checks your wallet,
      puts on a different coat,
          and goes.

Sentry

I can see you on the unlit landing
listening to the breathing of your boys
beyond the call of any other noise
or loyalty or outside understanding;

I can see the nerves that you're commanding
shot to hell by strafings of self-doubt,
and I can see exhaustion holding out
against the movement of your life's disbanding.

The landing is too dark and near to boys
who sleep too deep and warm among their toys
for this to be explained or understood;

I would meet your challenge if I could,
but there's a password that I can't conceive,
and you're the sentry no one can relieve.

Hypomania

Naked, you were, goose-pimpled and alone,
the evening that you climbed up Arthur's Seat
and gifted Edinburgh a bittersweet
atonal frenzy on your saxophone,

until you took that urge to meet with God
by running till you hit the speed of light,
so ran, ran hell-for-leather in the night,
your pell-mell thighs whipped on by a half-lob

boner – and almost met Him, fleetingly,
the moment when you belly-flopped the scree
to scourge yourself red raw from chin to toe.

At least you learnt to fly – three yards or so –
before the forces men have not invented
made your acquaintance. The sax was dented.

To a Waitress in India

A hip and wacky western coffee bar
with walls akimbo, riots of torn cloth,
eclectic tables randomly distressed
and purple pointy-titted *objets d'art*

suggests that one must travel long and far
to leave behind the hot designer froth
of cappuccino culture in the west –
much further than this town in India;

and what of you, your corporate fusion sari,
your earnest English as you fail to sell
this westerner a special cheesy dip?

Madam, you have been globalized, I'm sorry.
What can we do, but what we both do well –
your tired smile as I leave, my hefty tip?

Marathon Runner with Bob-hat

Your ankles are two torture victims squabbling
to be executed first, your shoulders are
a gallows that your arms are swinging from
still half-alive, your feet are cripples hobbling

over broken glass, your shins are instruments
of terror finely tuned, your mouth's a scar
ripped open at each step, your lungs are bombs
exploding in your chest, your ligaments

are chains that cut into your flesh, your hands
are spades to dig your grave, your knees are cars
crashing, your joints are mules that won't go on,
your forehead is a tightened iron band,

and you – you finish it in five hours flat.
You look a mad old fucker in that hat.

Must

We circle warily in Bewley's Bar,
in Biddingtons, at parties with your friends,
using public means for private ends,
knowing and not knowing how things are.

It lasts for months, a strange and bittersweet
confusion of one woman and one man –
(what makes you think it has more meaning than
two pigeons circling in a city street?)

until thank God I pull your knickers down
and it's resolved – how wonderful to drown
in it, the old imperative of love –

(but can't you see it has the nature of
those pigeons going at it in the dust,
which build their messy nests because they must?)

In Darkness, John

In darkness, John, at midnight and in bed,
you'll lie around your heart's dismissive beat
and under an anticipating sheet
grow very old, and exponentially,

until you are so old you will be dead.
Your bones will be astonishing and small.
The furniture will press against the wall.
Your children will be very far away.

The final dog you own will start to whine.
A neighbour's voice will hail you from the hall.
The doctor will arrive, but not in time.

The undertaker will be asked to call.
A ladybird will settle on your head
and walk your jaw-line, John, the day you're dead.

No Tongues

You've seen the coffee shop that's over there?
Well when you're walking past it, wear a hat.
Above it, from the window of that flat,
there's these two girls who shout abuse and swear,

and sometimes, so it's said, they even bare
their arses (wouldn't mind a look at that)
and once, as I was ambling by, they spat
warm gobs of spit across my face and hair.

Now I'm not one to boast, and yet I've known
a girl's saliva mingling with my own
on many a dark sweet sweaty breathless night,

so by and large I'm not averse to kissing,
and currently it's something that I'm missing –
but not with girls like that, from such a height.

Beam Me Up

You've seen those high-tech toilets on the trains,
the silent space-age panel opening to
admit you to a futuristic loo
of sensors, back-lit buttons, moulded drains

and woosh-dry flushes like the ones in planes?
The fittings are a soothing pastel hue
conducive to the things one has to do,
and if you're grimacing and having pains

a hologram of Charlotte Church appears,
and mops your brow, and calms your deepest fears…
All right, those last two lines I wrote were lies,

so read the final two for simple fact:
peeing is an ancient, low-tech act –
it doesn't need the Starship Enterprise.

Blackberrying

You've seen those berries in the superstore?
A hundred grams at £1.29?
Do virgins bathe them one by one in wine
then fly them (business class) from Ecuador

to get such prices? There's blackberries galore
not half a mile away! They freely line
the park, their taste as sharp and sweet and fine
as any berries mouths have watered for.

A superstore's okay for parents who
are drained with work and still have meals to do,
and cub-scout-ballet-lesson ferrying,

but mammies, daddies, just remember this:
your wee ones when they're grown won't reminisce
about the day you took them berrying

in Safeways.

The Tree

I saw a single silhouetted crow
deep in the centre of a wind-whipped tree,
black in an icy trap of twiggery,
cold on a night-bound mountainside of snow.

It was the fear of dying in the dark.
It was a speck of hope for one day more.
It was the only breathing thing I saw
in all the seven hours of my walk.

And did it know the living thing in me?
Or did it see a blue thing come and go
automatically across the snow?

Tonight I'll have my warm and human bed,
and there are forty years of me ahead
before I'll have to perch within that tree.

After the Documentary

We're sitting in the darkness of The End.
Now that the distant horrors have been screened
it's time to slip away into our clean
life, waiting for us like a guilty friend.

Some men were captured as I weighed the chore
of tackling that old plate-fused Camembert
inside the fridge, then tortured as I dared
to wonder what the hell my life is for.

The sombre credits roll, it's time to eat,
but not until The End's end will we go,
since something holds you back inside your seat,

as though there could be something else to know,
as though there could be something else to mourn.
There's nothing else. We die because we're born.

Bus Station in Winter

As the flapping anoraks cavort
round the grisly bodies of the thin,
and as throbbing lumpy legs support
slabs of fat wrapped up in folds of skin,
and as the unsavoury exhort
the unfortunate ones to give in,
buses wait, like colds that will be caught.

And a snuffling pensioner exists
anxiously in what is left to live,
and a lank-haired mother grips the wrist
of her horror shrill and talkative,
and I see a sad girl being kissed
by a cheating man she will forgive,
and the buses go, like chances missed.

Addiction

I thought about the ordinary Germans
and how they closed their eyes to genocide.
I thought about the priest, his tender sermons,
and thirty years of little boys who cried.

I asked myself the questions in the night
that won't be answered for eternity,
my sleep as distant as the absent light
whose darkness seemed the only certainty.

I wished I were among the chewing beasts
that need no cause to carry on or die,
but graze where grass with nothingness converges

far from pointless thoughts of how and why.
I think I am those Germans, and that priest,
who found distraction in their blackest urges.

Seduction on the 10.18

You sat beside her, crossed your legs, and mused
upon her face. Your trousers were too short,
your ankles bald and pasty, and I thought
I saw you tugging up your socks. She snoozed,

she dozed inside her beauty's lucky bed
while you sat on the end of it to wait,
and when she woke you didn't hesitate
but got stuck in with all the things you said.

That she got off the train with you still rankles.
I'd like to know what she was thinking of,
you might have dumped her after having sex,

you might have throttled her amazing neck.
Or maybe, as I write, you're both in love –
and you with stupid trousers, pasty ankles.

419

An email

Dear Friend, have no suspiciousments or fear.
My name is Budwa Charles, attorney to
the President Kabila of Zaire,
assassinated in attemptive coup.

My client (late) had trusted my good name
of (US) 50 million dollar stash.
No family is come forwarded to claim,
and now I must secure abroad the cash.

On you I have esteeming profile to
a triple 'A' of highest finance sense,
and would put half in best account you own,

and profit 12.5 per cent to you.
Please send, in speedy highest confidence,
the details of address and fax and phone.

Isn't It Time You Started Saving?

An advertisment

Thousands of our smiling clients know
it's sensible to put some cash aside!
"*I want my girl to be the kind of bride
who won't forget her wedding*" – Mr O.

"*When I retire, I'd really like to see
the famous lands I've dreamt of*" – Mrs Pugh.
Just send the coupon off and we'll tell you
how low our direct-debit scheme can be.

(NOTE: Past performance not indicative
of future yields, and gains may be short-lived;
the value of investments can go down

as well as up; initial joining fee.)
G.M. – "*We save a monthly twenty-pound,
and soon we'll get a new conservatory!*"

Particulars

A property description

Located in a much sought-after street,
this most impressive charming one-bed flat
with parking and communal garden at
the rear comprises living room complete

with laminated flooring (newly laid)
and striking reproduction fireplace,
a bedroom (double-glazed) with ample space
for storage and a step with balustrade

to en-suite bathroom with extractor fan,
plus well-appointed recently extended
kitchen-diner boasting open-plan

array of units with a splashback tile,
and all white goods concealed in "Shaker" style.
Early viewing highly recommended.

*

The Passion of King Edward IV for Elizabeth Gray

A *passage from Sir Thomas More's* History of King Richard III

Whom when the King beheld and heard her speke,
as she was both right fair and of good favour,
wel made and very wise, of moderate stature,
he waxed enamored on her and would seek

aside a privy talk, whose appetite,
when ones perceiued, she verteously denyed –
but that she did so wiseli dignifyed,
with so good manered wordes caste so right,

that kindled him the moreso she declined,
who wist herself too simple for his wife
yet demed herself too good for concubine,

and so the King – her constaunce as the spur
to him that had not else been nayed in life –
determined in all hast to mary her.

Outbreak (1995)

    A film review

People bleed to death from tip to toe
in old-style sleepy small-town Cedar Creek;
breakneck action scenes but plotting weak,
and Hoffman is too stiff as medico

Sam Daniels, the plucky army doc
whose quest to find a cure to save the life
of poor old Cedar Creek (and his ex-wife)
is – yes – a thrilling race against the clock.

With maverick hero, goofy sidekick and
a ruthless general set to nuke the town
(a stunning turn by Donald Sutherland),

director Wolfgang Petersen goes tearing
through every hammy cliché going down.
(Rated R, for violence, gore, and swearing.)

A Shakespeare Glossary, C.T. Onions

A book blurb

This indispensable analysis
of William Shakespeare's lexicon will be
an aid of such pronounced utility
as specialists can ill-afford to miss.

A one-time scholar with the OED,
in Dr Onions' scholarship we find
linguistic treasures of the playwright's mind
emancipated from obscurity.

Elizabethan studies being vast,
and thinking in the field advancing fast,
this new edition carefully collects

a comprehensively enlarged syntaxis.
OF RELATED INTEREST TO THIS TEXT:
Bertrand Evans, *Shakespeare's Tragic Practice*.

Fireworks

I like those ones that shriek into the dark
to cause the cowardice of Labradors,
I like it when a firework explores
the universe and wastes itself, a spark

merely for a moment in a black grate;
I like those ones reluctant to go off,
which fart across six feet of lawn, or cough
inside their milk bottles, or lie in wait

for uncle to investigate then BANG
they blow his hearing aid; I like those louts
over there, hilarious with drink, who hang

around for kicks, bangers stuffed in their pockets
like loaded guns or dicks to boast about.
Come on then, boys, amaze me with yer rockets.

Second Day in Bam

Some twenty thousand died,
the city upside down,
and other thousands lie
dying underground.

For now, no mention of
the high and holy power
of God's unbounded love,
nor where He was that hour;

we'll have to wait until
some lonely living man
is dug out of his den

before they'll speak again –
the churchmen, as they will,
about that miracle.

Man Going up a Hill for a Reason

a reason

a hill

and reached the place he went to – just the same,
he got there and turned back, it's such a shame,
the only answers were the ones which came:

that everything is everything it seems,
and people have evolved beyond their means,
and hills are meals where sheep must eat their greens.

Man Sun-bathing: Results Confirmed

Briefs briefer than the blank blink of his eyes,
skin like an elephant hide burnt russet,
he hooked his index fingers in his gusset
and tucked it snug between his balls and thighs,

then lay down on the lounger, calm, perplexed,
and legs akimbo like a stirruped mother,
watching the sun from one knee to the other,
that moves the earth from this day to the next.

this day

the next

What Fault Line?

What fault line was your love concocted on
when, cool as you like, as curt as a nod,
as unexpected as an act of God,
it folded into this oblivion?

I loved you and I love you and you've gone,
and so we've altered into you and me;
We were the world, and now I'm only sea
without your shores to break my monsters on.

You don't know me now, so please accept
these snapshots of the unimpressive views
across my landless waves of solitude:

I have a job at which I am inept,
perform indignities just as I choose,
and keep a little list of girls I've screwed.

Atkinson

I didn't go to where I should have gone
because of rumours that the wall had breached,
and soon I was so far beyond the reach
of all their threats – the madman Atkinson,

his tub-thump wife, his lisping hangers-on –
that I was stumbling on the very beach
of Atkinson's fine phrases when he preached.
That's when I saw the sea, and the horizon –

but not one altar, no, and not one steeple,
and not the scrolls, and not the sacred bells,
and not the godhead living with the people.

I watched the turquiose sea for seven mornings
and then came back, for there was nothing else,
and I was missing Atkinson's shrill warnings.

Thrush

I know about the feathered thrush that sings
before the dawn; and there are sanctioned lovers
wrapped together at that time in covers
hot and tangled, with all the peace that brings.

And I could envy men and women who
legitimately love, for they can stroll
down High Streets hand in hand, and lightly call
each other darling in the cashpoint queue.

But you're engaging in adultery,
and I – what the hell am I thinking of
these afternoons, sloping to you with my heart?

Our thrush is singing me to you to me,
and wakes us up at dawn, itchy and apart,
scratching at that sly old fungus, love.

Two Policemen at Dawn

The younger one has done it twice before,
the slow drive down a dull suburban street,
the squinting through the darkness from his seat
to check a number on a locked front door,

then parking at the kerb. It's ten to four,
and the older one, who hasn't done it yet,
says fuck, and fuck. He smokes a cigarette
to keep a boy alive five minutes more,

then raps the door the way a policeman should,
which has the woman bolting up in bed,
knowing at once her second-born is dead

– the son she'd cede the first for, if she could –
begging her husband to wake up, wake up,
shaking his body as the dogs erupt.

A Woman

Was I the only one who saw her cry?
She crossed me on the Mile, eyes raw and low,
went slowly grieving past the Netherbow,
a self-contained but desperate passerby.

Everybody's father has to die,
though whether hers had died I wouldn't know;
and lovers love us deeply, till they go,
but who's to say if hers had gone, or why?

More likely, as you say, her tears were
for smaller causes than the ones I state –
though I'm the one who saw the then of her,

and paused before I walked to where I went,
not knowing who she was nor what it meant –
and watched her disappear down Canongate.

Index of Titles